The Adventures of the Thug Puppies

By

Phyllis Stein Beal

Copyright © 2024 by Phyllis Stein Beal

All rights reserved. No part of this publication may be reproduced, distributed, or transmitted in any form or by any means, including photocopying, recording, or other electronic or mechanical methods, without the prior written permission of the publisher, except in the case of brief quotations embodied in critical reviews and certain other noncommercial uses permitted by copyright law.

Published by Hemingway Publishers

Cover design by Hemingway Publishers

ISBN: Printed in the United States

HEMINGWAY
PUBLISHERS

Dedication

"Dedicated to the memory of my husband, Cee Beal.

Your thug puppies loved you so much; you were the best human Daddy ever!"

Table Of Contents

Dedication 3

Finding Forever Home 6

Chapter 1 6

Going on Vacation 14

Chapter 2 14

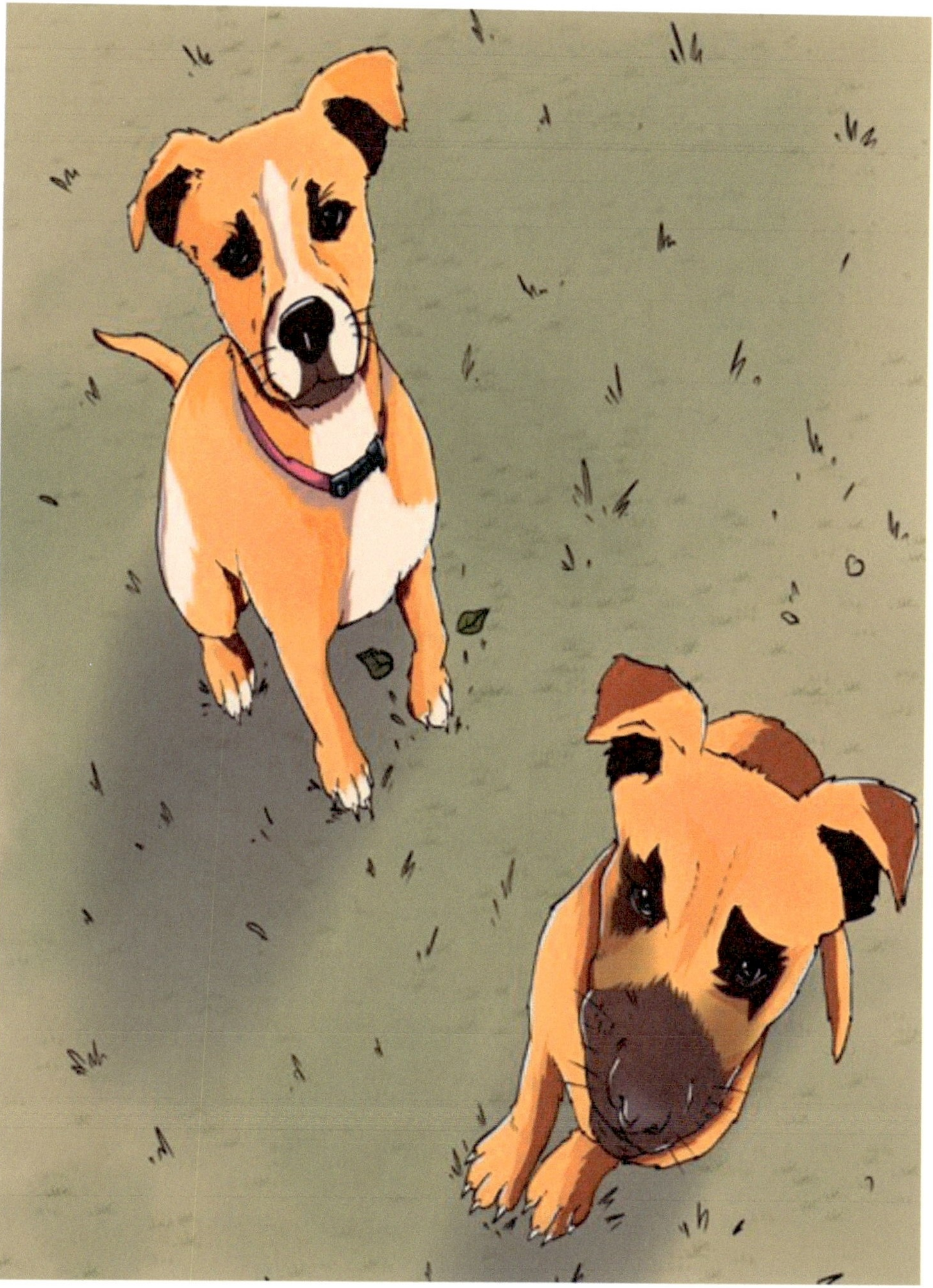

Finding Forever Home

Chapter 1

Mama Dog played with her puppies, Missy and Carmel, in the big yard. She taught them to fetch sticks and play with balls.

"Come, children, I have exciting news for you!"

"What, Mama, What?" The puppies ran to their Mama, tumbling and stumbling along the way.

"You are going to your forever home today."

"What is a forever home?" Missy asked.

"It is a wonderful place where you will have a warm bed, lots of balls and sticks, and cuddly stuffed babies. You will have good food and humans who will love you forever," Mama replied.

"I'm scared, Mama. I want to stay with you," Carmel cried.

"Don't be scared. Your forever humans chose you to love."

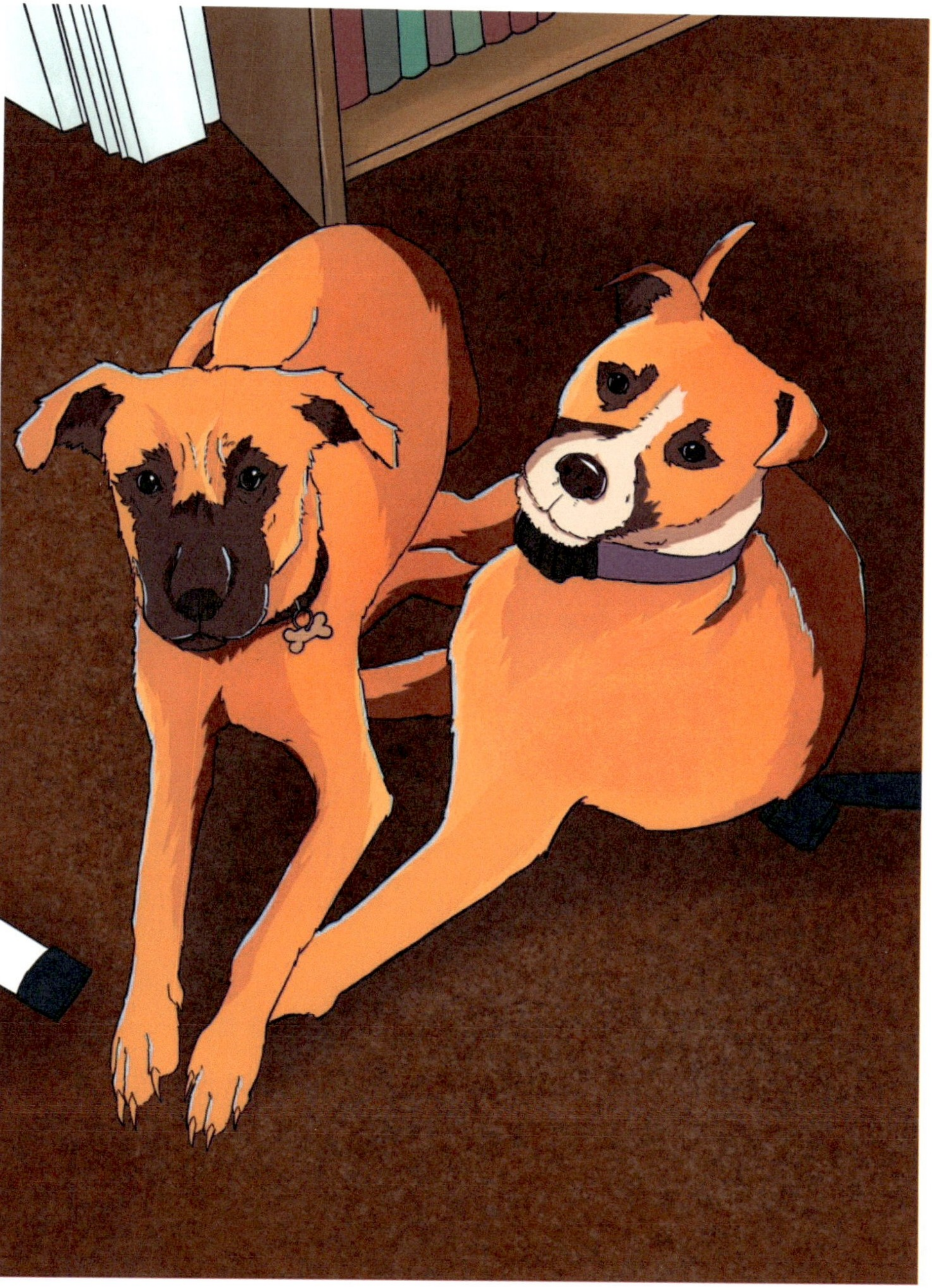

Mama Dog hugged and kissed her babies and told them to be good, brave puppies. She wiped away a tear as they went off with their humans.

The puppies ran through their new house and big fenced-in yard and played very hard. They were both happy to take naps in their fluffy new beds.

Missy and Carmel had a special toy box for their stuffed babies and toys. They took their toys out of the box and dragged them all over the floor. Daddy Human laughed and picked them all up.

Mommy Human brushed the puppies every day and took them for car rides. Their Humans taught them how to sit and stay and rewarded them with treats.

The puppies liked to wrestle-tussle in their big yard. Missy showed Carmel how to crawl through a hole in the big fence. But their Humans had been watching them and brought them back inside the wall.

As they grew up a little, they learned to climb the fence and run, run, run down the street. Daddy Human called, "Come back here, little thug puppies. It is dangerous for you to run down the street."

But they kept running.

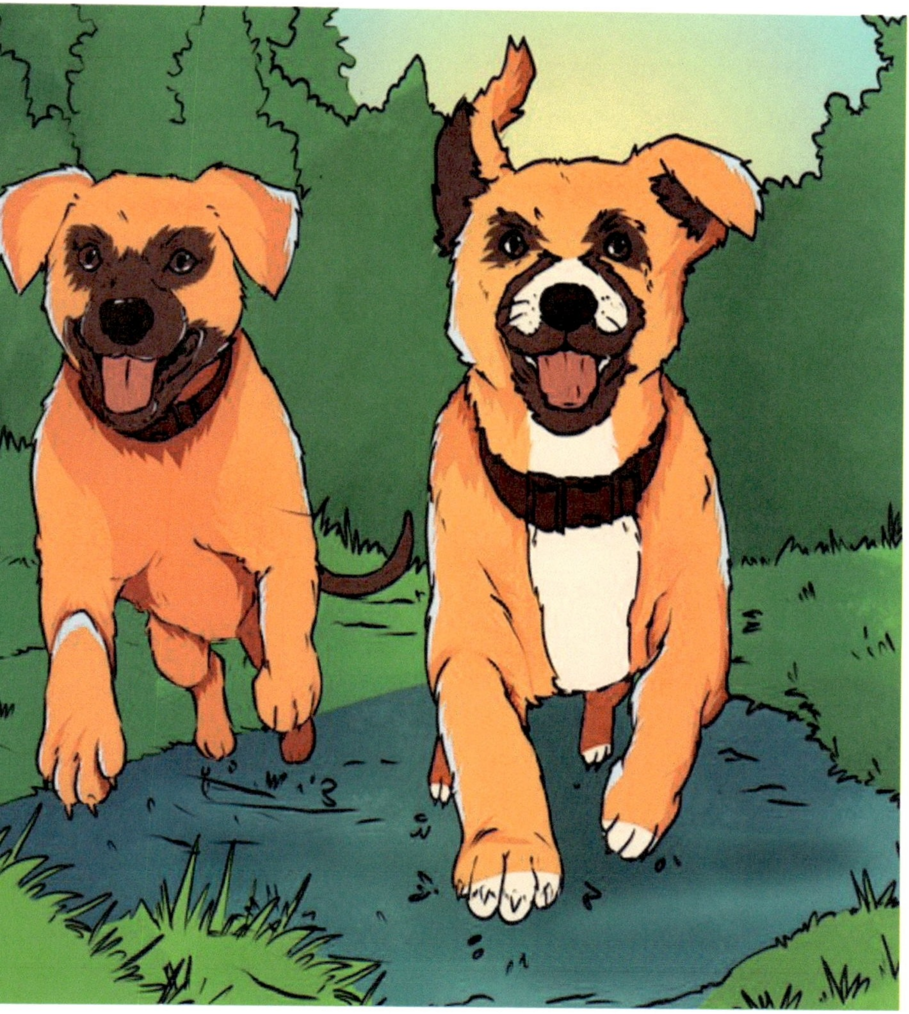

"Where is our forever home?" Carmel asked.

Missy said, "I will show you, Sissie." And off they went again, running like the wind.

Every time they went on a search for their forever home, their Humans found them and brought them home. They hugged and kissed the naughty thug puppies and told them, "This is your home now."

One day, in the summer, when the thug puppies were about six months old, they dug a hole under the fence, still trying to find their forever home.

They ran down the hill, past the trees, over the railroad tracks and very close to fast cars. They came to the big highway and were ready to cross it when a Stranger Human stopped them and held them close. Mr. Policeman drove up to the thug puppies and said, "Someone called me about runaway puppies." The Stranger Human told Mr. Policeman that she had called him.

Just then, Daddy Human arrived in the car. He said, "These are my puppies," But the Stranger Human would not let them go.

11

Daddy Human opened his hands and then called, "Come, Missy; come, Carmel," and they ran straight to Daddy Human, who hugged them and held them close.

Mr. Policeman agreed, "Yes, these are your puppies," and handed them over to Daddy Human.

When they got home, Daddy and Mommy Human hugged the thug puppies and told them that they loved them.

"This is your forever home, and you don't need to run away anymore," Mommy Human said.

The thug puppies licked and loved on their Humans and were so happy to have finally found their forever home.

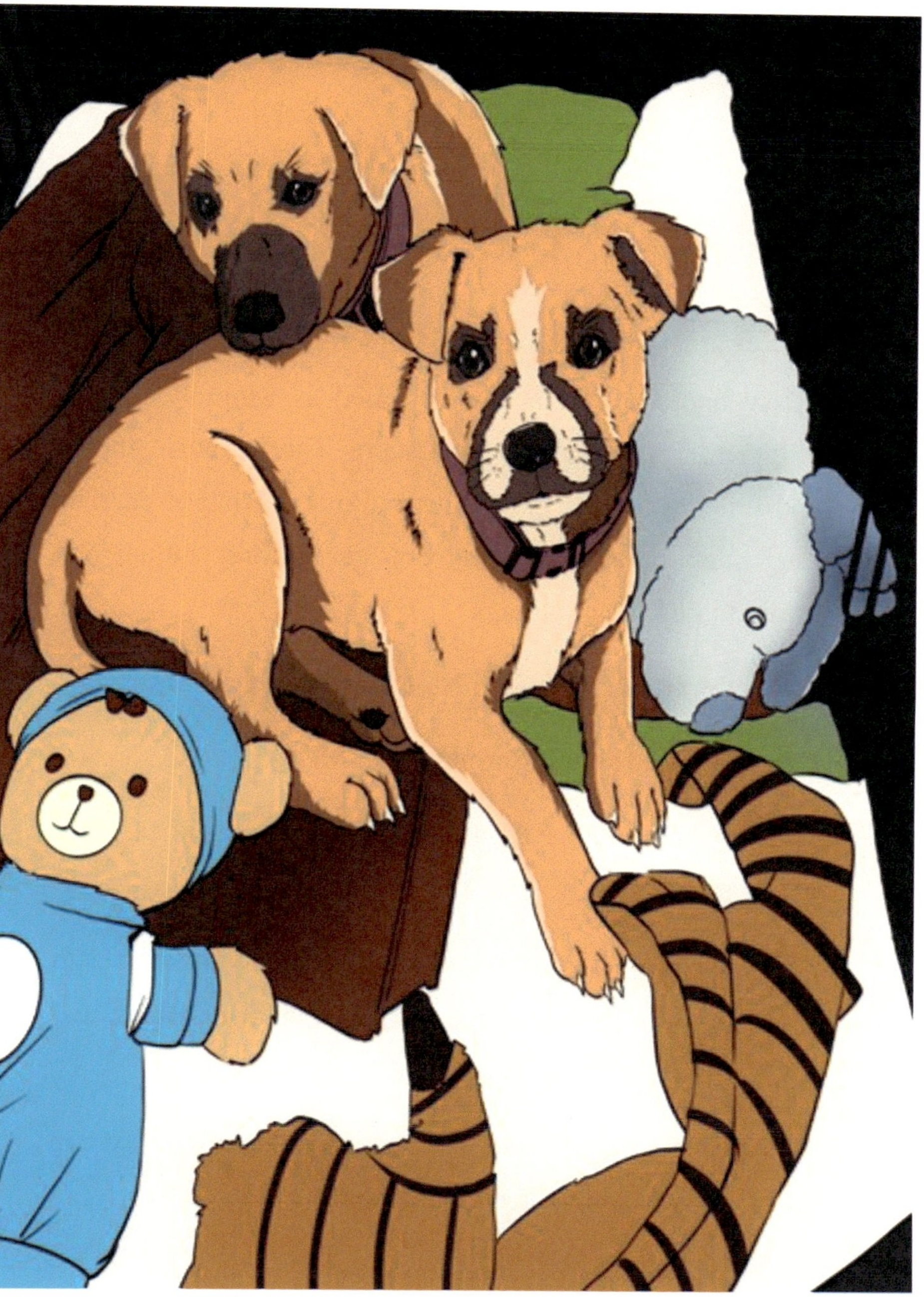

Going on Vacation

Chapter 2

Missy and Carmel sat and watched as Mommy Human dragged large items down the stairs. Thunk, thunk, thunk, and finally, she had gotten them into the living room. The thug puppies ran to the big objects, sniffing, biting, and trying to pull the big things.

"Missy! Carmel! Stop that! No chewing on the suitcases."

"What are suitcases?" Carmel asked Missy.

"I don't know, but I think Mommy Human will tell us," Missy said.

"We are going on vacation, and we will pack our clothes in here. The smaller suitcase is for your blankies, babies, and toys," Mommy Human explained to the puppies.

The thug puppies yipped and danced around. "Yay, we're going on vacation; going on vacation!"

"What's a vacation?" Carmel asked.

"Daddy Human and I are going away to a fun place for a few days. You girls will go to BowWow Kennels. It will be your own special vacation," Mommy Human said.

"Why can't we go with you?" Both thug puppies cried.

"Only humans can go there. But we will all go on a car ride together," Mommy Human explained.

The next few days, Mommy Human packed clothes, shoes, and books into the big suitcase. The thug puppies watched as she packed some of their stuffed babies into the smaller bag. Missy pulled out the toys as soon as Mommy Human packed them. She ran around the house with her toys.

"Bring them back, Missy," Mommy Human said, laughing as Missy tried to hide her toys. "I'm not taking your babies away. They are going with you."

When the big day finally arrived, Daddy Human loaded the suitcases, dog food, and treats into the car.

He opened the back door and went back inside to get the thug puppies.

When Missy and Carmel saw their leashes, they were so excited, jumping up and down. "We're going on vacation; going on vacation!"

"C'mon girls, jump into the car." Both Missy and Carmel jumped in the back seat in one leap!

The thug puppies loved riding in the car with their Humans. Such a fun adventure!

When they arrived at BowWow Kennels, Daddy and Mommy Human walked the puppies inside.

The noise and smells were frightening for Missy and Carmel. They pulled and tugged on their leashes. So many barking dogs!

Daddy Human put the thug puppies in a very large kennel. It had a small door that led out to a play area just for them.

Mommy Human put the blankies and favorite toys in with them. "Be good, girls; we will be back in a few days."

Missy and Carmel cried as their Humans left. Miss Lollywag, the kennel caretaker, tried to calm the puppies down and talked softly to them.

Still, Missy and Carmel sniffed and cried and tried desperately to escape.

"C'mon, Carmel. Let's get out of here and go on vacation with our Humans," Missy said.

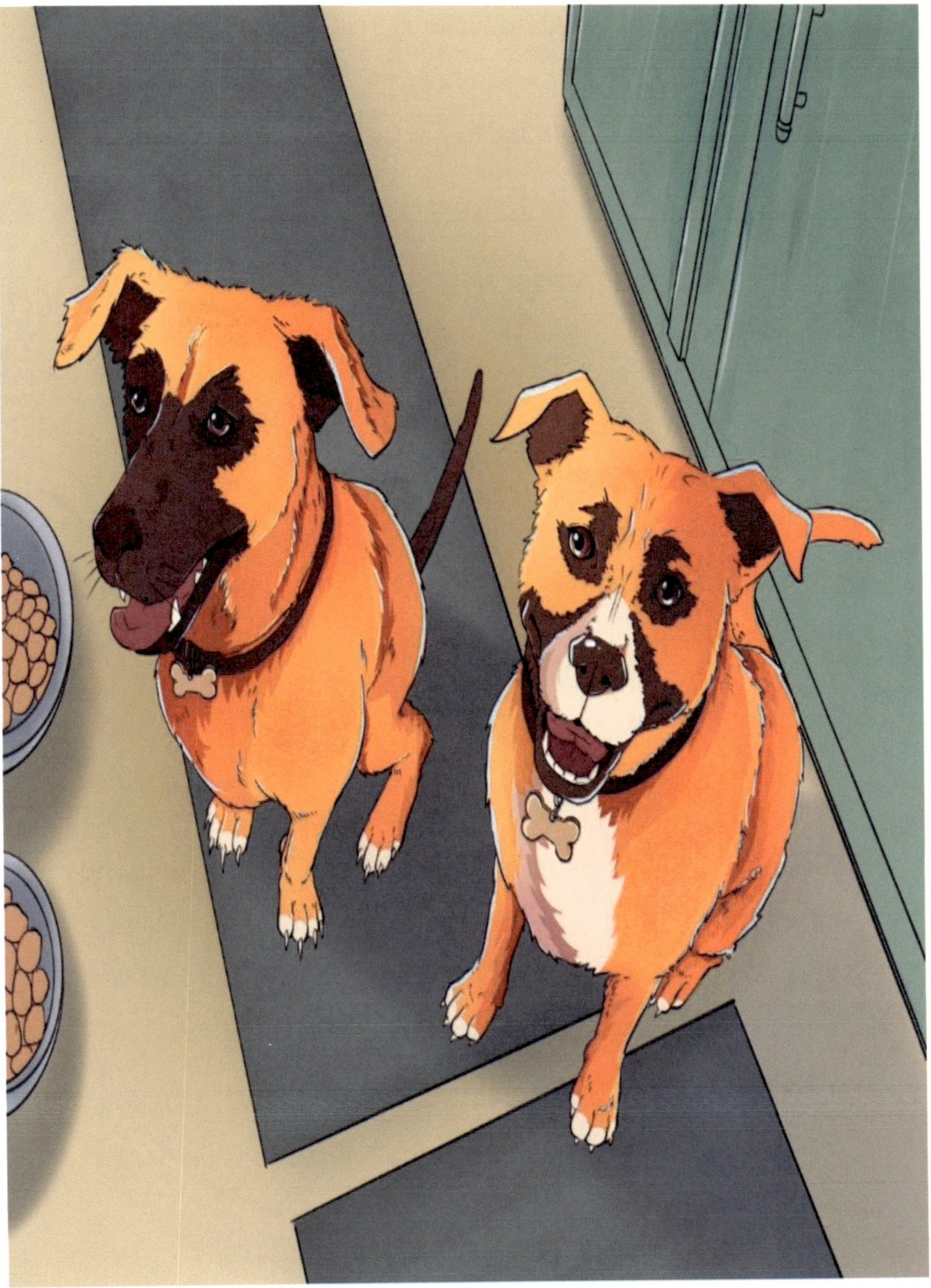

She jumped and tried to unlatch the kennel door, but it wouldn't budge. Again and again, she tried to undo the latch. Finally, she was able to unlock it!

"Yay! Let's go find our Humans."

As they started down the hallway, Seymour, a Great Dane, barked and said, "Take me with you. I don't want to stay here."

Biggie Small, a tiny Chihuahua, cried, "Take me, too!"

So, Missy tried and tried, and she was finally able to unlock both doors. Missy, Carmel, Seymour, and Biggie Small ran together down the long hallway toward the front entrance. But Seymour stopped and said, "Let's go the other way so Miss Lollywag doesn't see us."

They ran toward the back of the kennel and through a door that opened into a giant play yard. They had a wonderful adventure and played zoomies, wrestle-tussle, and hunted for sticks. The new friends were having so much fun they forgot about escaping. Suddenly, Miss Lollywag was standing in the doorway, hands on her hips.

"C'mon, boys and girls, fun times are over; let's go back to your kennels now."

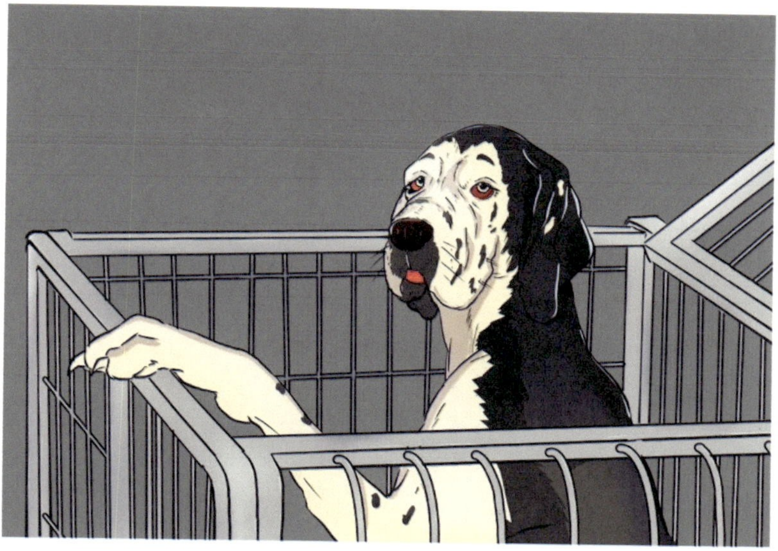

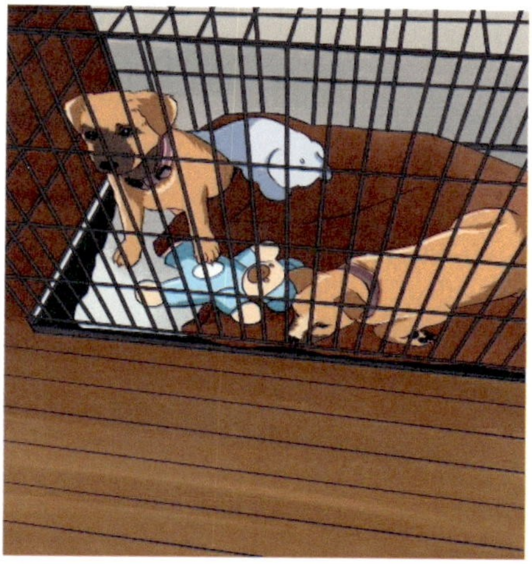

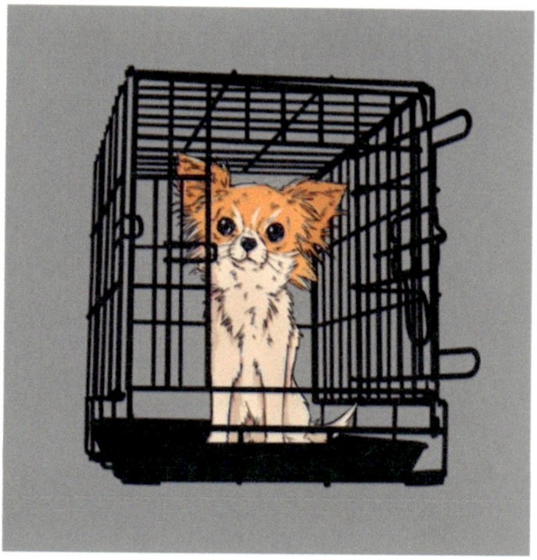

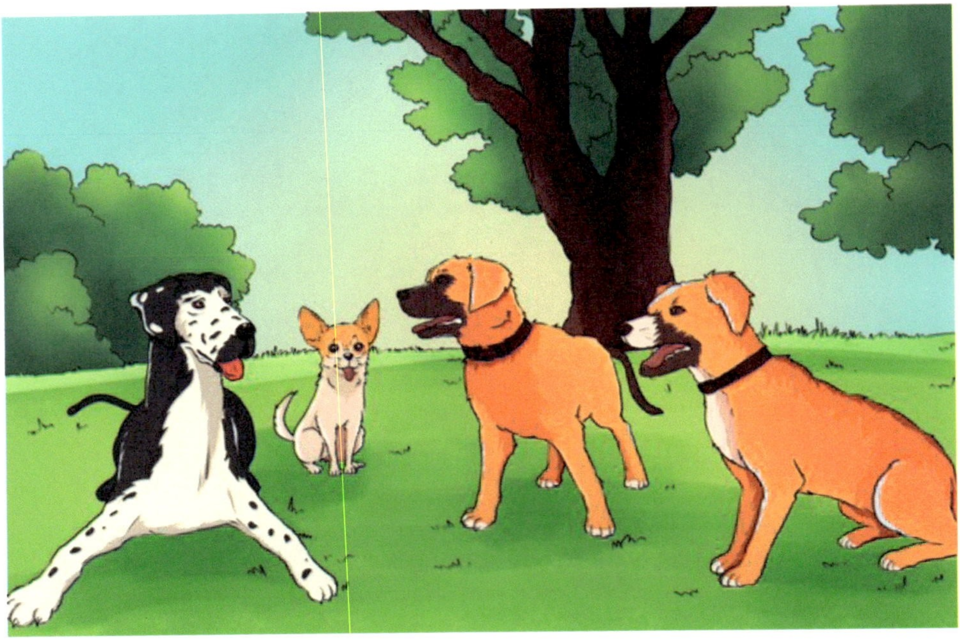

Missy, Carmel, and their friends, Seymour and Biggie Small, trotted back to their kennels. Miss Lollywag locked the doors, this time with two locks!

"Now, your Humans will be back soon. Stay put!" Missy and Carmel just looked at her with big, sad eyes. They lay down on their blankies and waited.

"Do you think Daddy and Mommy Human are coming back to get us?" Carmel asked Missy.

"I don't know," Missy said. "But vacation was fun when we were playing with Seymour and Biggie Small."

Early the next morning, there was a noisy commotion at the front door. And guess what?

Daddy and Mommy Human walked in, calling to their thug puppies, "C'mon babies, let's go home!"

The thug puppies jumped up and down with excitement! Seymour and Biggie Small woofed goodbye to their vacation friends. The thug puppies woofed back.

Missy and Carmel walked outside and jumped in their car.

"Yay, we're going home," they both yipped happily and sat like pretty statues in the back seat.

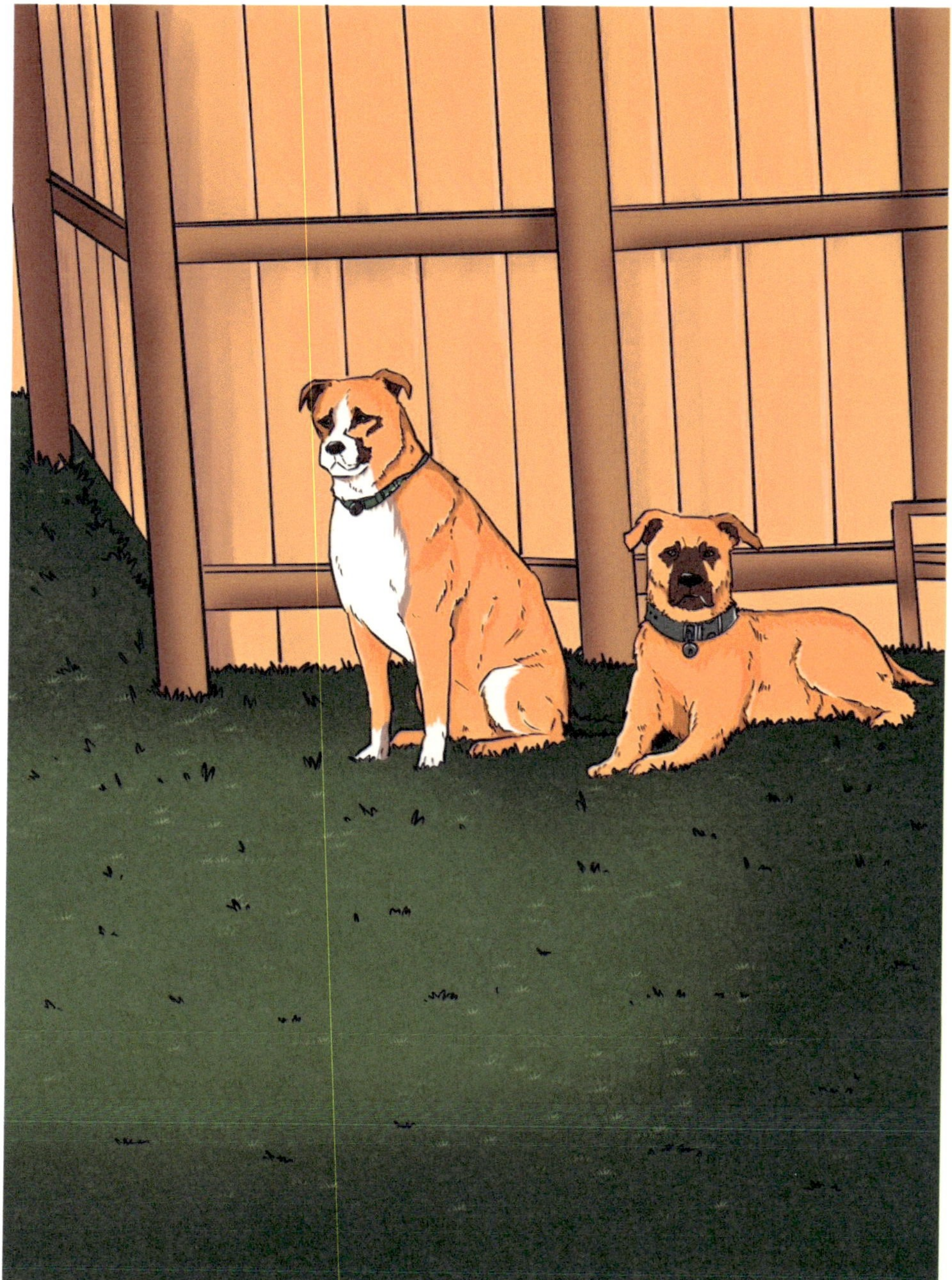

As soon as they got home, Missy and Carmel ran zoomies in their big yard, played wrestle-tussle, pulled their toys out of the toy box, and then happily curled up on their soft beds.

"We're home!"

And then they took a nap.

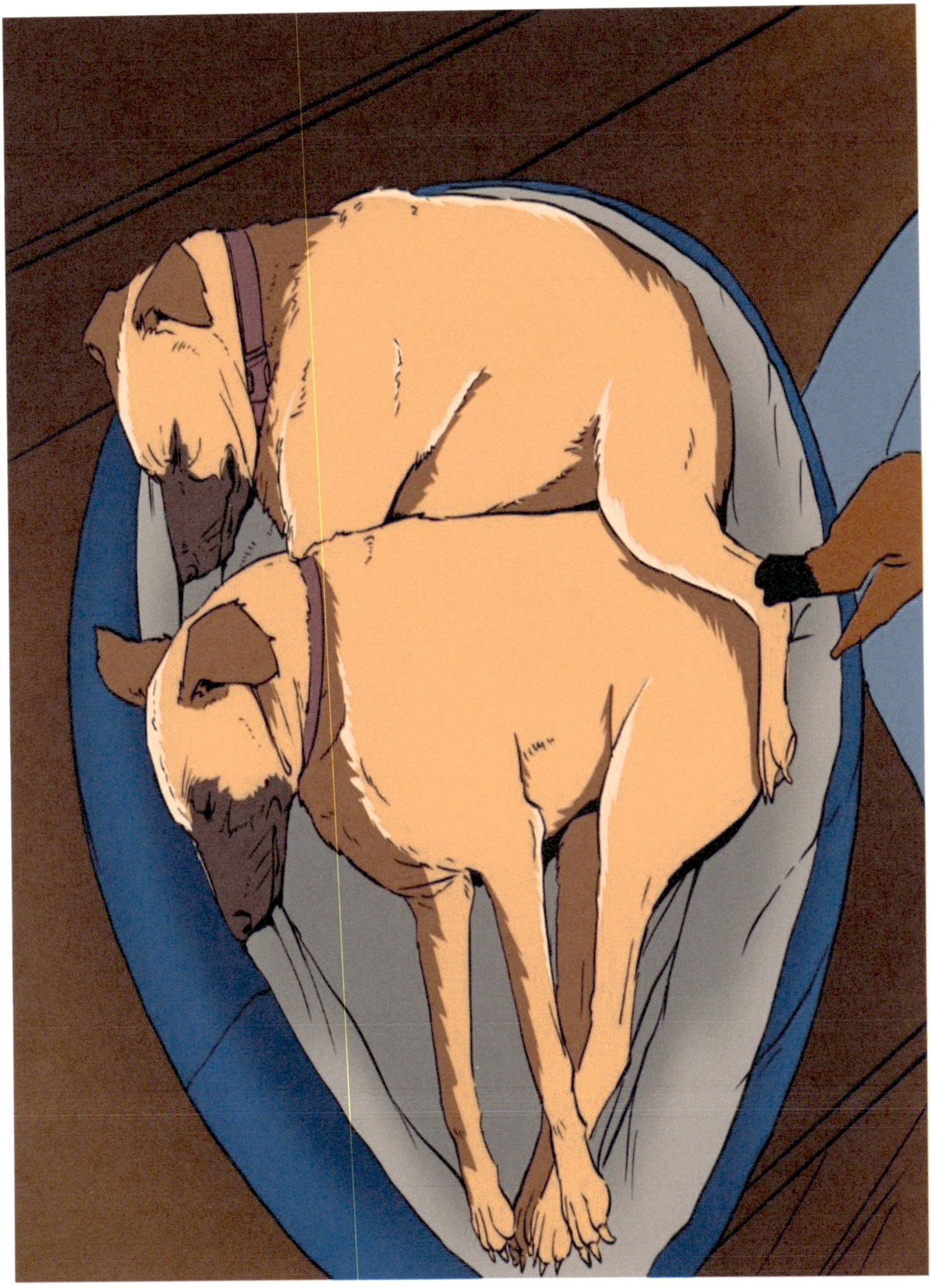

Made in the USA
Columbia, SC
17 March 2025